S0-CWR-158

Other giftbooks by Helen Exley:

Thoughts on... Being Happy
Thoughts on... Being at Peace
In Beauty May I Walk: Native American Wisdom
Bon Voyage!
The Best of Nature Quotations

Published simultaneously in 1997 by Exley Publications in Great
Britain, and Exley Giftbooks in the USA.
Copyright © Helen Exley 1997
The moral right of Helen Exley has been asserted.
Quotations selected by Helen Exley
Illustrated by Angela Kerr
Printed in China

12 11 10 9 8 7 6 5 4 3 2 1

ISBN: 1-85015-855-X

Exley Publications Ltd, 16 Chalk Hill, Watford,
Herts WD1 4BN, UK.
Exley Giftbooks, 232 Madison Avenue, Suite 1206,
NY 10016, USA.

seize
the day!

A Helen Exley Giftbook

EXLEY
NEW YORK • WATFORD, UK

Nothing is worth more than this day.

JOHANN WOLFGANG VON GOETHE

*If I had my life to live over... I would
perhaps have more actual troubles,
But I'd have fewer imaginary ones.*

NADINE STAIR

It is so hard for us little human beings to accept this deal that we get. It's really crazy, isn't it? We get to live, then we have to die. What we put into every moment is all we have....

GILDA RADNOR

Stars over snow,
And in the west a planet swinging
below a star –
Look for a lovely thing and you will find it,
It is not far – It never will be far.

SARA TEASDALE, "NIGHT"

Carpe diem, quam minimum credula a postero.
Seize the day, and put the least possible trust in tomorrow.

HORACE

You don't get to choose how you're going to die. Or when. You can only decide how you're going to live. Now.

JOAN BAEZ, FROM "DAYBREAK"

Eternity is not something that begins after you are dead. It is going on all the time. We are in it now.

CHARLOTTE PERKINS GILMAN

Give us grace, O God, to dare to do the deed which we well know cries to be done. Let us not hesitate because of ease, or the words of [people]'s mouths, or our own lives.

W.E.B. DU BOIS

When any one of us says: "I will live tomorrow," he indulges in a dangerous fantasy about living. The life that the dawn brings us is the only life we have.

VIMALA THAKAR

*Accept the pain, cherish the joy, resolve
the regrets; then can come the best of
benedictions – "If I had my life to do over,
I'd do it all the same."*

JOAN McINTOSH

Life engenders life. Energy creates energy.
It is by spending oneself that
one becomes rich.

SARAH BERNHARDT, IN "MADAME SARAH"

*A life of reaction is a life of slavery,
intellectually and spiritually. One must fight
for a life of action, not reaction.*

RITA MAE BROWN

For every person who has ever lived there has come, at last, a spring he will never see. Glory then in the springs that are yours.

PAM BROWN

I choose to inhabit my days, to allow my living to open me, to make me less afraid, more accessible, to loosen my heart until it becomes a wing, a torch, a promise.

DAWNA MARKOVA

I will not be just a tourist in the world of images, just watching images passing by which I cannot live in, make love to, possess as permanent sources of joy and ecstasy.

ANAÏS NIN

I had not loved enough. I'd been busy, busy, so busy, preparing for life, while life floated by me, quiet and swift as a regatta.

LORENE CARY, FROM "BLACK ICE"

Enjoy the blessings of the day... and the evils bear patiently; for this day only is ours: we are dead to yesterday, and not born to tomorrow.

JEREMY TAYLOR

Life itself is the proper binge.

JULIA CHILD

And whatsoever you do, do it heartily.

COLOSSIANS 3:23

I think it pisses God off if you walk by the color purple in a field somewhere and don't notice it.

ALICE WALKER

I wish I knew what people meant when they say they find "emptiness" in this wonderful adventure of living, which seems to me to pile up its glories like an horizon-wide sunset as the light declines.

EDITH WHARTON

What worth has beauty, if it is not seen?

ITALIAN PROVERB

Every year I live I am more convinced that the waste of life lies in the love we have not given, the powers we have not used, the selfish prudence that will risk nothing....

MARY CHOLMONDELEY

... if you really and sincerely and passionately want to do something (and wholeheartedly, with the whole of your sincerest self) it is by doing <u>that</u> that you will be most useful, will be giving the most, will be of most individual value.

ANNE MORROW LINDBERGH

I want to live only for ecstasy. Small doses, moderate loves, all half-shades, leave me cold. I like extravagance. Letters which give the postman a stiff back to carry, books which overflow from their covers, sexuality which bursts the thermometers.

ANAÏS NIN

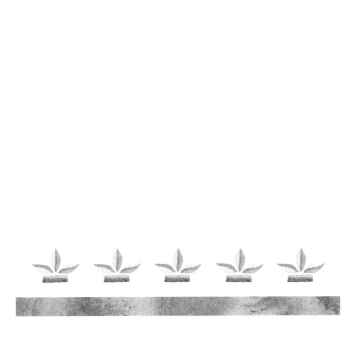

You can have anything you want if you want it desperately enough. You must want it with an exuberance that erupts through the skin and joins the energy that created the world.

SHEILA GRAHAM

It's only when we truly know and understand that we have a limited time on earth – and that we have no way of knowing when our time is up that we will begin to live each day to the fullest, as if it was the only one we had.

ELISABETH KÜBLER-ROSS

Gather ye rosebuds while ye may,
Old time is still a-flying:
And this same flower that smiles today
Tomorrow will be dying.

ROBERT HERRICK

Life is either a daring adventure or nothing.

HELEN KELLER

I believe that life should be lived so vividly and so intensely that thoughts of another life, or of a longer life, are not necessary.

MARJORY STONEMAN DOUGLAS

*A new life begins for us with every second.
Let us go forward joyously to meet it. We
must press on, whether we will or no, and
we shall walk better with our eyes before
us than with them ever cast behind.*

JEROME K. JEROME

It is time for every one of us to roll up our sleeves and put ourselves at the top of our commitment list.

MARIAN WRIGHT EDELMAN

With life I am on the attack, restlessly ferreting out each pleasure, foraging for answers, wringing from it even the pain. I ransack life, hunt it down.

MARITA GOLDEN

But warm, eager, living life – to be rooted in life – to learn, to desire to know, to feel, to think, to act. That is what I want. And nothing else. That is what I must try for.

KATHERINE MANSFIELD

If the engine whistles, let it whistle till it is hoarse for its pains. If the bell rings, why should we run? Time is but the stream I go a-fishing in.

HENRY DAVID THOREAU

To see a World in a Grain of Sand
And a Heaven in a Wild Flower,
Hold infinity in the palm of your hand
and Eternity in an hour.

WILLIAM BLAKE

It is time to come to your senses. You are to live and to learn to laugh. You are to learn to listen to the cursed radio music of life and to reverence the spirit behind it and to laugh at its distortions. So there you are. More will not be asked of you.

HERMAN HESSE

That it will never come again is what makes life so sweet.

EMILY DICKINSON

I have learned to live each day as it comes and not to borrow trouble by dreading tomorrow.

DOROTHY DIX

People do not live nowadays – they get about ten percent out of life.

ISADORA DUNCAN

... we live in the past or in the future; we are continually expecting the coming of some special moment when our life will unfold itself in its full significance. And we do not notice that life is flowing like water through our fingers.

FATHER ALEXANDER ELCHANINOV

Life was meant to be lived and curiosity must be kept alive. One must never, for whatever reason, turn one's back on life.

ELEANOR ROOSEVELT

[People] for the sake of getting a living forget to live.

MARGARET FULLER

Flow with whatever may happen and let your mind be free. Stay centered by accepting whatever you are doing. This is the ultimate.

CHUANG TSU

Make hay while the sun shines.

PROVERB

I expect to pass through this world but once, any good thing therefore that I can do, or any kindness that I can show to my fellow creature, let me do it now, let me not defer or neglect it, for I shall not pass this way again.

STEPHEN GRELLET

Write it on your heart that every day is the best day in the year.

RALPH WALDO EMERSON

Each day that I live I say to myself: the visible world is mine, use it, change it, but be quick, for the night comes all too fast and nothing is ever entirely finished, nothing.

GORE VIDAL

The biggest sin is sitting on your ass.

FLORYNCE KENNEDY

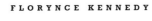

I will not die an unlived life.
I will not live in fear
of falling or catching fire.

DAWNA MARKOVA

They are committing murder who merely live.

MAY SARTON

*Security is when everything is settled,
when nothing can happen to you; security
is the denial of life.*

GERMAINE GREER

*How can you hesitate? Risk! Risk anything!
Care no more for the opinion of others, for
those voices. Do the hardest thing on earth
for you. Act for yourself. Face the truth.*

KATHERINE MANSFIELD

Everyone should have a chance at a breathtaking piece of folly at least once in his life.

ELIZABETH TAYLOR

I don't want to get to the end of my life and find that I lived just the length of it. I want to have lived the width of it as well.

DIANE ACKERMAN

Life is in the here and now, not in the there and afterwards. The day, with all the travail and joy that it brings to our doorstep, is the expression of eternal life. Either we meet it, we live it – or we miss it.

VIMALA THAKAR

Make voyages. Attempt them.
That's all there is.

ELAINE DUNDY

Do not linger to gather flowers to keep them, but walk on, for flowers will keep themselves blooming all your way.

RABINDRANATH TAGORE

Never say –
"One day I'll venture..." The moment is now.

PAM BROWN

When I'm old I'm never going to say,
"I didn't do this" or, "I regret that." I'm
going to say, "I don't regret a damn thing.
I came, I went, and I did it all."

KIM BASINGER